THE WAY EYE SEE IT
CYCLOPS TELLS ALL

by Nancy Loewen
illustrated by Ryan Pentney

Cyclops' Sheep: "SERIOUSLY, HE'S GOTTEN A WOOLLY BAAAD RAP!"

PICTURE WINDOW BOOKS
a capstone imprint

In Greek mythology Odysseus was a brave and cunning leader. After winning the Trojan War, he and his men set sail for their homes across the sea. Along the way they landed on the island of the Cyclopes. The men entered and were later trapped inside a cave belonging to Polyphemus and his herd of sheep. Much to Odysseus' horror, Polyphemus ate two of the men the first night, two the next morning, and two the second night.

Odysseus came up with a plan. He offered Polyphemus strong wine. When the giant fell asleep, the remaining men stabbed him in the eye with a sharpened log. The next morning the blind Polyphemus let out his sheep one at a time. He checked their backs, making sure his prisoners weren't riding the sheep out of the cave. But the men were clinging to the bellies of the sheep, undetected, and escaped.

That's the classic version of the story.

But how would Polyphemus tell it?

My name is Polyphemus. Ever since I can remember, I've dreamed of getting off this island and seeing the world. I want to climb mountains, buy souvenirs at all the tourist spots, and dance until dawn—do all the things those little two-eyed humans do!

But it will never happen now—especially after what happened with Odysseus. I should've known better. Sometimes I'm just not a very smart Cyclops.

The day started like any other day. I took my sheep out to pasture in the morning and came back in the evening. But when I got home, there was an odd smell in my cave. Humans! And there they were: a dozen or so men huddling in the dark.

A phrase from my childhood sprang into my mind.

You are what you eat.

You are what you eat.

You are what you eat.

Here was my big chance! If I ate humans, maybe I would become human. Then I could travel the world!

lit my evening fire. The men shrieked when they saw me in the light.

One brave man stepped forward. "We are Greek soldiers, on our way home from war. Please, in the name of Zeus, be kind to us."

"Of course," I replied. "You must be hungry. I'll make up a cheese plate!"

We ate together, and I gave them all clean towels and handmade soaps. When the cheese was gone, it was time for me to make my move. I was a little nervous, of course. I'd never eaten humans before. What if they were stringy? What if their little fingers and toes got stuck in my throat?

"This has been lovely," I said. "And now I have a favor to ask. I would like to eat two of you. Any volunteers?"

A few of the men laughed. "I've never met a Cyclops with a sense of humor," one of them said.

"I'm serious," I said. "You are what you eat, and more than anything, I want to be human. So I thought I'd start with two and see how it goes."

Then they *all* laughed.

It looked like I'd have to do this the hard way—hard for them, anyway.

"I beg your pardon," I said. And before they knew what was happening, I grabbed two men and took a big bite of each. They tasted like chicken.

The men were stunned. Then they started yelling. "That's just an old saying!" they cried. "You can't take it literally!"

I washed down my meal with a big sheepskin full of milk. "Look, I can see that this upsets you, and I'm sorry," I said. "But I just *have* to be human. It's my destiny. Good night!"

The next morning I checked to see if I'd changed. My clothes seemed a little baggy—could I be shrinking? And was it just me, or were my hands less hairy?

"I think this is working!" I said cheerily to the men. "Who's next?"

This time the men ran around the cave like we were playing tag. Eventually I caught two of them. They tasted like chicken too, with a hint of handmade soap.

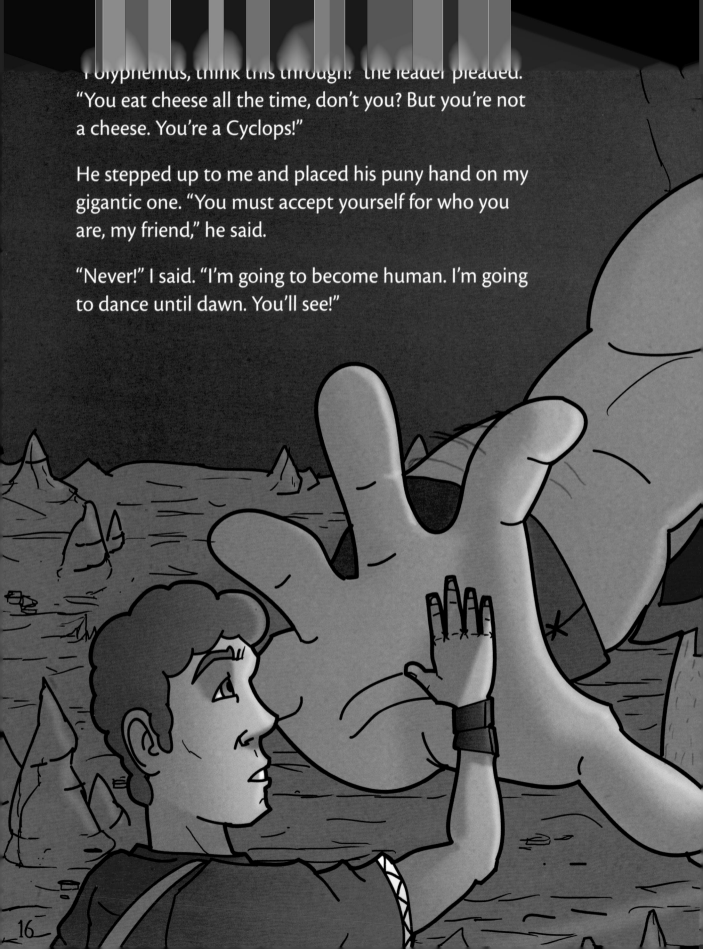

"Polyphemus, think this through!" the leader pleaded. "You eat cheese all the time, don't you? But you're not a cheese. You're a Cyclops!"

He stepped up to me and placed his puny hand on my gigantic one. "You must accept yourself for who you are, my friend," he said.

"Never!" I said. "I'm going to become human. I'm going to dance until dawn. You'll see!"

I took my sheep out for the day.
When I returned in the evening,
I ate two more men.

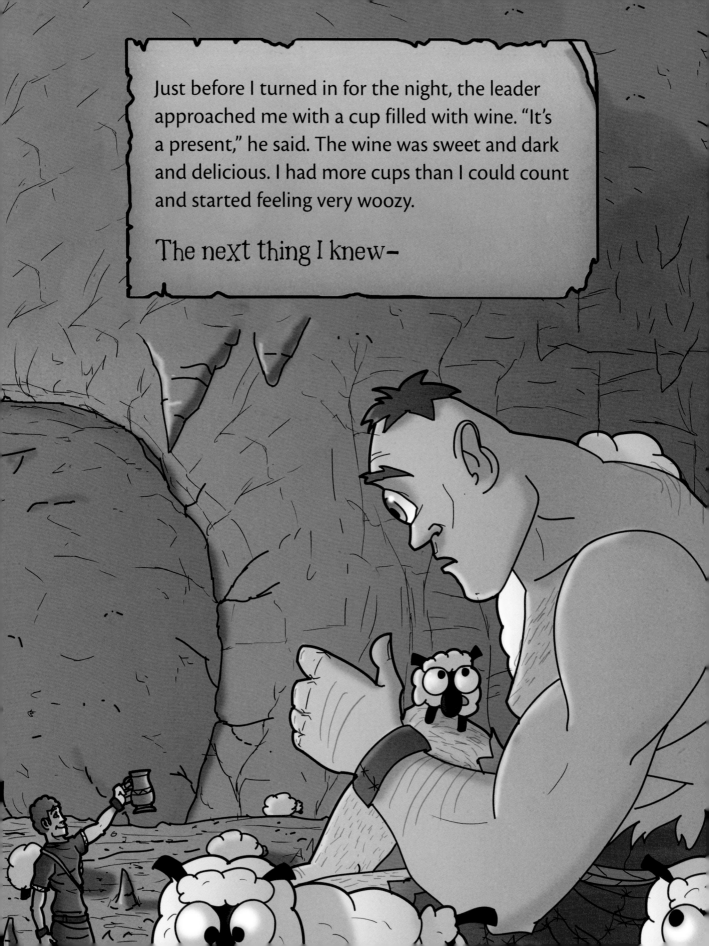

Just before I turned in for the night, the leader approached me with a cup filled with wine. "It's a present," he said. The wine was sweet and dark and delicious. I had more cups than I could count and started feeling very woozy.

The next thing I knew–

"OUCH! YIKES! OWIE OWIE OWIE!"

I'd been poked in the eye with a stick! I could barely see!

I hollered and hopped around so much that the milk in the milking pails turned into butter.

Finally I collapsed into an exhausted sleep.

In the morning, I saw no reason to be polite. (In fact, I saw nothing at all.) "I'll eat every last one of you if I have to!" I said, thrusting my hands out blindly and hoping to catch someone. But I came up empty.

When my sheep started getting restless, I rolled back the boulder and let out one sheep at a time. I felt their backs, just to be sure the men hadn't gotten any funny ideas about riding them out of the cave.

Slowly I made my way down to the beach and splashed water on my poor, aching eye.

Someone was calling to me. "Hey there, you one-eyed oaf! If anyone asks who hurt your eye, tell them it was I, Odysseus, King of Ithaca!"

"Come back!" I begged. "I'll forgive you if you just let me eat a couple more men!"

"Oh, for the love of Zeus!" Odysseus said. "YOU ARE WHAT YOU EAT just means that if you want to be healthy, you have to eat healthy foods!"

My heart sank.

"You mean there's no chance at all that I'll become human?"
I asked.

"NO!" the men all shouted.

I was so disappointed and angry that I picked up all the
rocks I could find and flung them blindly into the sea.

All I wanted was to see the world. Now I can barely see my own island.

So you can feel as sorry as you want for the soldiers I ate and their friends. I understand.

But save a little sympathy for me too, OK?

Critical Thinking Using the Common Core ★ ★ ★ ★ ★

This version of the classic Greek myth is told by Polyphemus, from his point of view. If Odysseus told the story, what details might he tell differently? What if one of Polyphemus' sheep told the story from its point of view? (Integration of Knowledge and Ideas)

A proverb is a short saying that expresses a truth or offers advice. By the end of the story, Polyphemus learns the real meaning of the proverb "You are what you eat." Consider the following proverb, and explain its meaning: "The pen is mightier than the sword." How about "The squeaky wheel gets the grease"? (Integration of Knowledge and Ideas)

In this version of the story, Polyphemus doesn't eat Odysseus' men to be mean. Explain his reason for eating them, and describe the ways he shows the men kindness. (Key Ideas and Details)

Glossary ★

Cyclops—a one-eyed monster from Greek mythology

destiny—a special purpose

literally—at face value; actually

mythology—old or ancient stories told again and again that help connect people with their past

point of view—a way of looking at something

Trojan War—a 10-year war during which the Greeks tried to win control of the city of Troy

version—an account of something from a certain point of view

Zeus—the king of the gods

Read More

Cooper, Gilly Cameron. *Odysseus and the Cyclops.* Graphic Greek Myths and Legends. Milwaukee: World Almanac Library, 2007.

Meister, Cari. *Odysseus and the Cyclops: A Retelling.* Mankato, Minn.: Picture Window Books, 2012.

Smith, Charles R., Jr. *The Mighty 12: Superheroes of Greek Myth.* New York: Little, Brown, 2008.

Internet Sites

FactHound offers a safe, fun way to find Internet sites related to this book. All of the sites on FactHound have been researched by our staff.

Here's all you do:

Visit *www.facthound.com*

Type in this code: 9781479521807

Super-cool stuff!

Check out projects, games and lots more at
www.capstonekids.com

Thanks to our advisers for their expertise, research, and advice:

Susan C. Shelmerdine, PhD, Professor of Classical Studies
University of North Carolina, Greensboro

Terry Flaherty, PhD, Professor of English
Minnesota State University, Mankato

Editor: Jill Kalz
Designer: Lori Bye
Art Director: Nathan Gassman
Production Specialist: Danielle Ceminsky
The illustrations in this book were created digitally.

Picture Window Books are published by Capstone,
1710 Roe Crest Drive, North Mankato, Minnesota 56003
www.capstonepub.com

Library of Congress Cataloging-in-Publication Data
Loewen, Nancy, 1964–
 Cyclops tells all : the way eye see it / by Nancy Loewen ; illustrated by Ryan Pentney.
    pages cm.—(Nonfiction picture books. The other side of the myth.)
 Summary: "Introduces the concept of point of view through the Cyclops Polyphemus'
retelling of the classic Greek myth 'Odysseus'"—Provided by publisher.
 ISBN 978-1-4795-2180-7 (library binding)
 ISBN 978-1-4795-2955-1 (paper over board)
 ISBN 978-1-4795-2937-7 (paperback)
 ISBN 978-1-4795-3316-9 (eBook PDF)
 1. Cyclopes (Greek mythology)—Juvenile literature. I. Pentney, Ryan, illustrator. II. Title.
 BL820.C83L64 2014
 398.20938'01—dc23

                              2013032208

photo credit: Hugo-Gunn Photography

About the Author

Nancy Loewen writes fiction and nonfiction for
children and young adults. Recent awards include:
2013 Oppenheim Toy Portfolio Best Book Award
(*Baby Wants Mama*); 2012 Minnesota Book Awards
finalist (*The LAST Day of Kindergarten*); and 2010
AEP Distinguished Achievement Award (Writer's
Toolbox series). She's also received awards from
the American Library Association, the New York
Public Library, and the Society of School Librarians
International. Nancy holds an MFA in creative
writing from Hamline University. She lives in the
Twin Cities area of Minneapolis – St. Paul.

Look for all the books in the series:

CYCLOPS TELLS ALL: THE WAY EYE SEE IT
MEDEA TELLS ALL: A MAD, MAGICAL LOVE
MEDUSA TELLS ALL: BEAUTY MISSING, HAIR HISSING
PANDORA TELLS ALL: NOT THE CURIOUS KIND

Printed in the United States of America in Brainerd, Minnesota.
092013   007770BANGS14